T0342622

THE WISDOM OF OZ

AUSTRALIAN APHORISMS
FROM THE PROFOUND
TO THE PROFANE

Black Inc.

Published by Black Inc.,
an imprint of Schwartz Publishing Pty Ltd
Level 1, 221 Drummond Street
Carlton VIC 3053, Australia
enquiries@blackincbooks.com
www.blackincbooks.com

National Library of Australia
Cataloguing-in-Publication entry:
The wisdom of Oz.
9781863959889 (hardback)
Aphorisms and apothegms.
Quotations, Australian.

Extract from 'The Meaning of Existence' in
Poems the Size of Photographs © 2002 by Les Murray.
Reprinted with permission of Les Murray.

Extract from 'We Are Going' in *My People*
© 1970 by Oodgeroo Noonuccal. Reprinted with
permission of John Wiley & Sons.

Cover and text design by Peter Long

Printed in China by 1010 International.

An aphorism worthy of its name requires truth, surprise and concision. What it can never be is a homily. In compiling these quotes, we looked not only for lasting truths, but also for a touch of self-deprecation, an admission of fallibility, an honest comment that might cost political points. Although a few of the quotes in this collection don't exactly fall into the rarefied category of an aphorism, each speaks in a pithy way to a truth about the Australian character. They are also often brilliant and amusing in their laconic Australian cynicism. They might not all be Thoreaus or Emersons, but we rejected a great number of Aussie quotes, from many a collection, to select these gems.

The book opens with Kerry Packer's famous profanity: 'I've been to the other side and let me tell you, son, there's fuckin' nothing there.' Pronounced after his heart stopped beating for a minute or two, this is a rare example of the profane promoted on the cover. We are sure, given our national character, that there are countless other wonderful profanities that have slipped out of Aussie mouths, but by their nature they weren't recorded in the 'proper' collections of quotes.

By dint of prominence, if not necessarily talent, politicians are over-represented in quote books, and this one is as guilty as the rest. But we have taken care to adhere to our stipulations about truth, surprise and concision.

Malcolm Turnbull may be clever, but he's often prolix. And when he says, 'I believe that politicians should speak the truth all the time. Invariably there will be occasions when you make statements that are factually incorrect due to an error,' he is obviously bullshitting. He is ingratiating himself with the electorate. It's political talk. You won't find it in this book.

But we have happily included, 'When politicians offer you something for nothing, or something that sounds too good to be true, it's always worth taking a careful second look.' Here, Turnbull is being candid. He is telling us the truth.

'That's what being in the working class is all about – how to get out of it.' Neville Wran said that. It's in with bells on. It's fresh and honest, without even a whiff of ulterior motive.

But when Bill Shorten says, 'I relish the opportunity to talk about what I believe to be every Australian's right – a good, safe job with proper pay and conditions,' he doesn't get a look in. We might believe him, but he has given us a homily. Bill never drops his guard, and he does not appear in this collection.

And what to do with Tony Abbott? He has said some choice things:

We just can't stop people from being homeless if that's their choice.

Jesus knew that there was a place for everything and it's not necessarily everyone's place to come to Australia.

I don't think it's a very Christian thing to come in by the back door rather than the front door.

Aboriginal people have much to celebrate in this country's British heritage.

Oh, such silly stuff. This is the opposite of the wisdom promised in the title. You won't find him in these pages.

Nor John Howard. Not because of a position on his politics, but because he was so earnest, self-righteous and self-serving. He never let us in on any uncomfortable truths, and we read this as dishonesty – even if he did say, 'Truth is absolute, truth is supreme, truth is never disposable in national political life.' We don't believe you, John.

Compare Howard and Abbott to Ben Chifley, who said, 'Never is liberty more easily lost than when we think we are defending it.'

Our first prime minister, Edmund Barton, has also been left out. He had this to contribute to the wisdom of the ages: 'The doctrine of the equality of man was never intended to apply to the equality of the Englishman and the Chinaman.'

We hope this clarifies the vetting process. This is a little book about truth, in a world defined by insidious lies.

Enjoy!

I've been to the other side
and let me tell you, son,
there's fuckin' nothing there.

Kerry Packer,

after he was technically
dead for a few moments

Ah well, I suppose it has
come to this ... Such is life!'

Ned Kelly,

before he was hanged

Shoot straight, you bastards!
Don't make a mess of it!

Harry 'Breaker' Morant,

executed soldier and poet

It is not that I fear death.

I fear it as little as

to drink a cup of tea.

Ned Kelly

It's dead easy to die;
it's the keeping on living
that's hard.

Douglas Mawson

Many young people
die of old age.

F.J. Mills ('The Twinkler'),

Square Dinkum (1917)

It's very tiring, being so old.

But I do love living.

Dame Elisabeth Murdoch,

at 102

I know this beach like
the back of my hand.

Harold Holt's last words

No expedition has ever started under such favourable circumstances.

Robert O'Hara Burke

Australia is a lucky country,

run by second-rate people

who share its luck.

Donald Horne

For inclusion in the [Australian] history syllabus, you have to die a miserable death, preferably alone in the desert… The best heroes are losers.

Richard Glover

The most gratifying thing about death is that you won't have to get up in the morning.

The Lone Hand magazine (1907)

Everything comes – too late –

for him who waits.

A.G. Stephens,

The Bookfellow (1912)

The past is so reliable,
so delightful and
the best place to live.

Barry Humphries

We know we cannot live in the past, but the past lives in us.

Charles Perkins

People who sit tight usually remain where they are.

F.J. Mills ('The Twinkler'), *Dinkum Oil* (1917)

The world will not wait for us.

Bob Hawke

Nationalism is both a vital medicine and a dangerous drug.

Geoffrey Blainey

Australians will never acquire a
national identity until
enough individual Australians
acquire an identity of their own.

Patrick White

Australia formed me,
I must be an Australian.

Christina Stead

We turned our backs on the
purifying waters of self-sacrifice.

Billy Hughes,
'On the issues at stake' speech,
London, 17 March 1916

I love Australia – I think.

Barry Humphries

There is no disguising a
Young Liberal's haircut.

Don Watson

Australia is wonderful place,
but it's wonderful in spite of its
current politics.

Martin McKenzie-Murray

No inferiority complex ever
found a place in the true
Australian creed of life.

Former Governor-General
Sir Isaac Isaacs,
New Year message,
January 1936

Australia is a huge rest home,

where no unwelcome news

is ever wafted on to

the pages of the worst

newspapers in the world.

Germaine Greer

New Zealanders who emigrate to Australia raise the IQ of both countries.

Former New Zealand Prime Minister **Robert Muldoon**

God bless America.

God save the Queen.

God defend New Zealand

and thank Christ for Australia.

Russell Crowe

It's the best country to get out of
that I was ever in.

Henry Lawson

You can be tops in Australia and be unheard of everywhere else.

Barry Gibb

In a way, Australia is like
Catholicism. The company is
sometimes questionable
and the landscape is grotesque.
But you always come back.

Thomas Keneally

Any boss who sacks a worker for
not turning up today is a bum.

Bob Hawke,

after the historic victory

of *Australia II* in the

1983 America's Cup

To live in Australia
permanently is rather like
going to a party and dancing
all night with your mother.

Barry Humphries

No man is a hero in
his own country.

Sir John Monash

No wars are unintended
or 'accidental'.

Geoffrey Blainey

I don't care a damn for your loyalty when you think I am right. The time I want it is when you think I am *wrong*.

Sir John Monash

The standard you walk past is
the standard you accept.

**Lieutenant General
David Morrison**

The structures that separate
civilisation from disorder
are thin and fragile.

Ross Garnaut

When the war process breaks
down, peace will be imminent.

Robert B. Mackay

Villains are rarely simple men.

Inga Clendinnen

Winning needs no explanation,
and losing has no alibi.

Greg Baum

This is not a message
to politicians.
They are not listening.

Erik Jensen

on the *Saturday Paper*'s
Change the Date campaign

Never sing in chorus,
if you want to be heard.

J.F. Archibald

Never is liberty more easily
lost than when we think we are
defending it.

Ben Chifley

Today, words.

Tomorrow, sticks and stones.

And the day after that?

Phillip Adams

I've never seen anyone
rehabilitated by punishment.

Henry Lawson

The truth is always libellous.

George Finey

.

It's a sign of your own worth
sometimes if you are
hated by the right people.

Miles Franklin

It isn't what they say about you,

it's what they whisper.

Errol Flynn

Our conscious destruction
of a planet friendly to
humans and other species
is the most significant
development in history.

Robert Manne

Remember, good planets
are hard to find.

Mick Fogg

Our world is a web of
interdependencies
woven so tightly it
sometimes becomes love.

Tim Flannery

There is only one place for any fur coat, and that is on the back of an animal.

Peter Singer

Everything except language

knows the meaning of existence.

Trees, planets, rivers, time

know nothing else.

Les Murray,

'The Meaning of Existence',

Poems the Size of Photographs

(2002)

The scrubs are gone,

the hunting and the laughter.

The eagle is gone,

the emu and the kangaroo

are gone from this place.

The bora ring is gone.

The corroboree is gone.

And we are going.

Oodgeroo Noonuccal,

'We are Going', *My People*

(1970)

If it moves, shoot it;
if it doesn't, chop it down.

Bush saying

Failure to act appears to
favour the present but it
certainly prejudices the future.

Barry Jones

Women are vital to us
maintaining our capability
now and into the future.
If that does not suit you,
then get out.

**Lieutenant General
David Morrison**

Could women have ever
descended to such depths
of misery and degradation
if women had a right in
making the laws for women?

Mary Lee

I believe every woman should have the right to live in a home free of deadly weapons.

Elizabeth Evatt

Supermarkets stand condemned
as symbols of man's
inhumanity to women.

Phillip Adams

I will not be lectured
about sexism and misogyny
by this man. I will not ...
Not now, not ever.

Julia Gillard

to Tony Abbott,

9 October 2012

Disappointment and adversity
can be catalysts for greatness.
There's something particularly
exciting about being the hunter,
as opposed to the hunted.
And that can make
for powerful energy.

Cathy Freeman

No, I don't run men down,
but I run down their vanity.

Louisa Lawson

It's no fun being a bluestocking
in a family of jockstraps.

Colleen McCullough

I think that testosterone
is a rare poison.

Germaine Greer

Revolution is the festival
of the oppressed.

Germaine Greer

In Australia,

not reading poetry

is the national pastime.

Phyllis McGinley

To think clearly
in human terms
you have to be
impelled by a poem.

Les Murray

A good book ... leaves you
wanting to reread the book.
A great book compels you
to reread your own soul.

Richard Flanagan

The greater the artist,
the greater the doubt.
Perfect confidence is
granted to the less talented
as a consolation prize.

Robert Hughes

Great literature is like moral
leadership: everyone
deplores the lack of it,
but there is a tendency to
prefer it from the safely dead.

Shirley Hazzard

Nothing they design ever
gets in the way of a work of art.

Robert Hughes

In Australia, the Man Booker
is sometimes seen as
something of a chicken raffle.

Richard Flanagan

Fiction is life

with the dull bits left out.

Clive James

Man is a predatory animal,
and this aspect of his nature
is nowhere better suited
by environment than
in the world of politics.

Dame Enid Lyons

When politicians offer you
something for nothing,
or something that sounds
too good to be true,
it's always worth taking
a careful second look.

Malcolm Turnbull

Always back the horse
named self-interest, son.
It'll be the only one trying.

Jack Lang

I like that horse Divide
and Rule. I've done that for
twenty years.

Arthur Calwell

That's what being in the
working class is all about –
how to get out of it.

Neville Wran

One man and a dozen fools
would govern better
than one man alone.

Ben Chifley

Politics is both fraud and vision.

Donald Horne

We'll keep the bastards honest.

Don Chipp

Leadership is not about
being nice. It's about
being right and being strong.

Paul Keating

Good economics
is good politics.

Paul Keating

The best way to help the poor
is not to become one of them.

Lang Hancock

God is making commerce

His missionary.

Joseph Cook

All I can see is my own,

and all I can't see is my son's.

John Batman

I am on the side
of the underdog, except when
I am on the side of the rich.

Errol Flynn

Always be an opportunist.

Richard Pratt

Nature abhors a profit.

Morry Schwartz

I'm not tied to any
particular political line.

John Hewson

I find a fence a very
uncomfortable place
to squat my bottom.

Bob Hawke

It is better to be defeated on principle than to win on lies.

Arthur Calwell

Sometimes you can have
competing election promises.

Malcolm Fraser

Never take any notice of
anonymous letters,
unless you get a few thousand
on the same subject.

Sir Robert Menzies

One thing about bureaucrats
is that they never swallow
their young. Leave them
alone and you'll find them
increasing every year.

Sir Robert Menzies

Do you know why I
have credibility? Because I
don't exude morality.

Bob Hawke

It is not always the highest
talent that thrives best.
Mediocrity, with tact,
will outweigh talent oftentimes.

Joseph Cook

The reaction to being the first
female prime minister
does not explain everything
about my prime ministership,
nor does it explain nothing
about my prime ministership.

Julia Gillard,

on losing the leadership

The day after I finished being prime minister, starting to pack my office, I took a call from Paul Keating, who said to me, 'We all get taken out in a box, love. Sorry, sorry to hear about you. We all get taken out in a box, love.' And never a truer word was spoken.

Julia Gillard and **Paul Keating**

I think personal diplomacy has caused a lot of mischief and harm ... The almost pathetic belief of some foreign ministers [is] that, if they had lunch with someone and called him by his Christian name, they have changed the fundamental facts of relationships between nations.

Sir Paul Hasluck

The most intense hatreds
are not between political parties
but within them.

Phillip Adams

The only person you resent
is yourself.

John Hewson

People die because they find

living too painful.

Malcolm Fraser

Pain is truth;

all else is subject to doubt.

J.M. Coetzee

If I have not lost my mind
I can sometimes hear it
preparing to defect.

Patrick White

I had always thought that
sorrow was the most
exhausting of the emotions.
Now I knew that it was anger.

Helen Garner

Panic has been with us from the start. It's so Australian.

David Marr

Fear can do

terrible things to a man.

A.B. Facey,

A Fortunate Life (1981)

I never allow of any difficulties.
The great secret of being
useful and successful is
to admit of no difficulties.

Sir George Gipps

The secret of solitude

is that there is no solitude.

Joseph Cook

Of all my wife's relations
I like myself the best.

Joseph Cook

Underwear is such

an emotional thing.

Elle Macpherson

I want to catch Mr Whitlam
with his pants down.

Malcolm Fraser

Flynn is not always in.

Errol Flynn

The tragedy of machismo
is that a man is
never quite man enough.

Germaine Greer

Remorse is the period between
one night and another.

George Blaikie

Don't worry about the world coming to an end today. It's already tomorrow in Australia.

Charles M. Schulz

My man, I don't want justice,

I want mercy.

Billy Hughes

to his portrait painter

Life wasn't meant to be easy.

Malcolm Fraser